Joseph Bruchac

by Margaret Morgan
illustrated by Rob Mancini

Harcourt

SCHOOL PUBLISHERS

Printed in China

ISBN 10: 0-15-351297-0
ISBN 13: 978-0-15-351297-1

Ordering Options
ISBN 10: 0-15-351211-3 (Grade 1 Advanced Collection)
ISBN 13: 978-0-15-351211-7 (Grade 1 Advanced Collection)
ISBN 10: 0-15-358028-3 (package of 5)
ISBN 13: 978-0-15-358028-4 (package of 5)

4 5 6 7 8 9 10 0940 15 14 13 12 11 10 09

Joseph Bruchac grew up with his
Grandma and Grandpa. There were lots of
beautiful plants and hills where they lived.

Grandma had many books. She
liked to read, and so did Joseph.

Joseph did things with Grandpa, too. They liked to go up to the hills where it was quiet.

4

Joseph's family had a shop. Joseph liked to help in the shop. Many people came to the shop and talked with friends. They liked to tell Joseph tales.

Now Joseph tells his own tales.
He likes writing about many things.
He lives and does his writing in the
house where he grew up.

Joseph has made a lot of books.
Many people know his name and read
his books.

Joseph likes his work very much.
He likes writing and telling his tales
to people.